Affidavits and Letters for the Real Estate Office

By Ramsattie Mahadeo

authorHOUSE®

AuthorHouse™
1663 Liberty Drive
Bloomington, IN 47403
www.authorhouse.com
Phone: 1-800-839-8640

First published by AuthorHouse 9/9/2009

ISBN: 978-1-4490-2556-4 (sc)

Printed in the United States of America
Bloomington, Indiana

This book is printed on acid-free paper.

This book was written with the intent of giving the proper legal letters and documents that applies in the Real Estate Law Office. Please note that the Law Firms in this book is fictional and is should be used as a guideline on how you should format your own letter heads. It should be used as a sample, along with all the figures in this book. The letters are a guideline on the proper way to direct a letter in a real estate transaction.

About the author, Ramsattie Mahadeo is a Legal Administrative Assistant and Paralegal, and owns her own firm called Liberty Paralegal. She is a Guyanese-Canadian and has been in the law field since 2001. Ms. Mahadeo graduated in the top of her class and is an advocate for human rights and justice in the community she currently resides in, Toronto. In my many years of practicing in the Legal field, I came across numerous lawyers and law firms who were interested in my book, however, I told them that it was a package deal, that I came along with the book. Now, I can say its not a package deal, you can now purchase the book. Remember these are just the guidelines on how a proper real estate transaction procedure would occur. You need to change the dates, the law firms, the vendor and purchasers information and the address of the properties that you are dealing with. As a legal secretary and a real estate lawyer, you will find this book to be very helpful in your practice of Law. If you are interested in ordering any books, please contact me thru email: ramsattie01@yahoo.ca

This book is dedicated to everyone who is in the real estate field..

BILL OF SALE AND WARRANTY

TO: Nicholas Windsor Cain and Stephanie Denise Cain, purchasers

AND TO: Michael, Eliad & Redford, solicitors for the purchasers

RE: Cain Purchase from Abel, 2 Brothers Road, York, Lot 11, Plan 9614

BILL OF SALE

IN CONSIDERATION of the closing of the above transaction and other good and valuable consideration, we set over, transfer, and assign unto Nicholas Windsor Cain and Stephanie Denise Cain all our right, title, and interest in all chattels, fixtures and equipment as set out in the agreement of purchase and sale and all other permanent fixtures now on the property and belonging to the vendors.

We hereby covenant and warrant that the said chattels, fixtures, and equipment are free and clear of all charges/mortgages, liens, and encumbrances, that we are entitled to sell and convey title to same, and that the same will be left on the premises on the closing of this transaction in good working order.

WARRANTY

We warrant that the subject premises have not been insulated with urea formaldehyde insulation material, and that there are no work orders or deficiency notices outstanding against the property or conditions that would give rise to such orders or notices. This warranty shall survive the closing of this transaction.

CANADIAN RESIDENCY

We warrant that when we agreed to sell the lands and premises in this transaction to the transferees, we were not, nor do we intent to be, prior to the closing of this transaction, non-residents of Canada within the meaning and for the purposes of the Income Tax Act of Canada.

Dated at _____ on _____, 200____.

_____

Jason Abel

_____

Jessica Abel

MICHAEL, ELIAD & REDFORD
BARRISTERS AND SOLICITORS
869 SENECA LANE
TORONTO, ONTARIO M6K 1F6

JOSEPH A. MICHAEL
DAVID W. ELIAD
ROBERT B. REDFORD
MARGARET T NESH

REFERENCE NO._____

Today's Date, 200___

Castles & Sands
Barristers and Solicitors
Suite 900
205 Portage Street
Markham, Ontario
L3R 3G3

Attention: Mr. Raymond G. Castles

Dear Mr. Castles,

Re: Cain purchase from Abel
      <u>2 Brothers Road, York, Lot 11, Plan 9614</u>

We act for the purchasers in the above transaction and understand you act for the vendors.
Our clients wish to take title as follows:

CAIN, Nicholas Windsor	date of birth:	June 16, 1966
CAIN, Stephanie Denise	date of birth:	July 13, 1968

Joint tenants

Our client's address for service will be the same as the property they are purchasing.

Please let us have the draft transfer, survey and statement of adjustments soon.

Yours truly,

Michael, Eliad & Redford

Robert B. Redford

rm

MICHAEL, ELIAD & REDFORD
BARRISTERS AND SOLICITORS
869 SENECA LANE
TORONTO, ONTARIO M6K 1F6

JOSEPH A. MICHAEL
DAVID W. ELIAD
ROBERT B. REDFORD
MARGARETT NESH

REFERENCE NO._____

Today's Date, 200___

Consumers Gas
500 Consumers Road
P.O. Box 650
Scarborough, Ontario
M1K 5E3

Ladies and Gentlemen,

Re: Cain purchase from Abel
      2 Brothers Road, York, Lot 11, Plan 9614

We act for the purchaser of the above transaction which closes on March 17, 2002. Please advise whether the property is served by your company and if your company has any account or contract with respect to equipment on the premises.

If the property is served by you, would you kindly advise if there are any arrears in respect of, or relative to, the property.

Further, if the property is served by your company, please arrange a meter reading for (Month and Year), and forward the final bill to Castles & Sands, Barristers and Solicitors, Suite 900, 205 Portage Street, Markham, Ontario L3R 3G3, attention: Mr. Raymond G. Castles. After (Month and Date), your records should be amended to show Mr. Nicholas and Mrs. Stephanie Cain as the new owners, and bills should be sent to them at the property address.

We enclose our cheque for $10.70 to cover your service fees.

Yours truly,

Michael, Eliad & Redford

Robert B. Redford
rm
Encl

MICHAEL, ELIAD & REDFORD
BARRISTERS AND SOLICITORS
869 SENECA LANE
TORONTO, ONTARIO M6K 1F6

JOSEPH A. MICHAEL
DAVID W. ELIAD
ROBERT B. REDFORD
MARGARET T NESH

REFERENCE NO._____

Today's Date

The Treasurer
Tax Department
City of York
2700 Eglinton Avenue West
Toronto, Ontario
M6M 1V1

Ladies and Gentlemen,

Re: Cain purchase from Abel
      2 Brothers Road, York, Lot 11, Plan 9614

We act for the purchaser in the above transaction which closes (Insert Date). We would appreciate a tax certificate for the above property setting out;

(1) All charges for realty taxes now outstanding against the subject property, including taxes for the current year.

(2) Any local improvement charges.

(3) Any charges for work orders, snow shoveling, demolition, hydro, water, or other public utility or charges under the Telephone Act, the Fire Marshall's Act, the Public Health Act or The Weed Control Act.

(4) Any charges or special rates under the Tile Drainage Act.

(5) Any other charges forming a lien by the municipality against the property.

We enclose our cheque for $20.00, to cover fees.

Yours truly,

Michael, Eliad & Redford

Robert B. Redford
rm
Encl.

MICHAEL, ELIAD & REDFORD
BARRISTERS AND SOLICITORS
869 SENECA LANE
TORONTO, ONTARIO M6K 1F6

JOSEPH A. MICHAEL
DAVID W. ELIAD
ROBERT B. REDFORD
MARGARET T NESH

REFERENCE NO._____

Today's Date 200___

Mr. and Mrs. David Solomon
96 Atlantic Avenue
Toronto, Ontario
M2V 2H6

Dear Mr. and Mrs. Solomon:

Re: Your sale to King, 100 Sisyphus Road, North York

We have now completed your sale of the above property and give you our report as follows:

Statement of Adjustments

Enclosed is a copy of the statement of adjustments for which adjustments were calculated as of (Insert Date). On closing, we turn over a transfer/deed of the premises made pursuant to the direction of the purchasers in favour of Sydney Haden King and Renee Pamela King. In return, we received from the purchasers' solicitors a certified cheque for _____, payable to our firm, in trust, as per your direction, which represented the balance due on closing as per the enclosed statement of adjustments. The cheque was deposited in our trust account the same day, and the transfer/deed was also registered that day.

As can be seen from the statement of adjustments, you were credited with the sale of the property in he amount of _____, and the purchaser was credited with the deposit monies of _____.

Taxes

For the purpose of adjustments, the taxes wee estimated to be _____. Since your share of the taxes amounted to _____ and you had paid _____ on this account, you received credit in the statement of adjustments in the sum of _____. After accounting for the foregoing adjustments, the purchaser was required to pay the balance due on the closing in the amount of _____.

Mr. and Mrs. David Solomon
Page 2
Today's Date

Real Estate Commission

You agreed to pay the real estate agent a commission of _____ percent of the sale price or _____. This amount is subject to GST and the total commission account was _____. It was deducted from the deposit of _____ and the balance of _____ was to be paid directly to you by the real estate agent. Id you do not receive these funds in a timely manner, please let me know, and I will pursue the matter on your behalf.

Account

Our enclosed account and ledger statement show you how we handled the money on closing. We also enclose our trust account cheque in the amount of _____ payable to David Solomon and Susanna Solomon, representing the balance of the monies we received on closing.

Enclosures

1. Copy of the transfer/deed

2. Statement of adjustments.

3. Direction regarding the taking of title.

Thank you for giving us the opportunity to serve you in your sale. Please call us with any questions.

Yours truly,

Michael, Eliad & Redford

Robert B. Redford

rm

Encl.

JOSEPH A. MICHAEL
DAVID W. ELIAD
ROBERT B. REDFORD
MARGARET T NESH

REFERENCE NO._____

Today's Date

Hydro Commission
Customer Accounts Department
1652 Keele Street
Toronto, Ontario
M6M 3W1

Ladies and Gentlemen,

Re: Cain purchase from Abel
      2 Brothers Road, York, Lot 11, Plan 9614

We act for the purchaser in the above transaction which closes on _____.
Would you please advise if there are any arrears of hydro rates affecting the above noted
property, or if there are any contracts, rental or otherwise, for equipment belonging to you on
the property.

Please arrange for the meter to be read on _____, and forward the final bill to
Castles & Sands, Barristers and Solicitors, Suite 900, 205 Portage Street, Markham, Ontario,
L3R 3G3, attention Mr. Raymond G. Castles. After _____, your records should be
amended to show Mr. Nicholas and Mrs. Stephanie Cain as the new owners, and bills should
be sent to them at the property address.

We enclose our cheque for $10.70 to cover your service fees.

Yours truly,

Michael, Eliad & Redford

Robert B. Redford
rm
Encl.

MICHAEL, ELIAD & REDFORD

BARRISTERS AND SOLICITORS
869 SENECA LANE
TORONTO, ONTARIO M6K 1F6

JOSEPH A. MICHAEL
DAVID W. ELIAD
ROBERT B. REDFORD
MARGARET T NESH

REFERENCE NO._____

Today's Date

Dyss Trust Company
55 Rodeo Drive
Toronto, Ontario
M2K 1T1

Attention: Ms. Alexandra Kirkev, Lending Officer

Dear Ms. Kirkev:

Re: Cain purchase from Abel
      2 Brothers Road, York, Lot 11, Plan 9614
      First Charge/Mortgage, Loan No. 080101

Please find enclosed our final report on title and the registered duplicate charge/mortgage of land registered _____, as Instrument No. TB423649.

As we advised you, the best evidence that the property is free from encroachment and claims for adverse possession is an up to date survey. In the absence thereof, it is usual practice for the vendor to provide a sworn declaration that they have reviewed the old survey and that the property complies with the survey and there have been no claims for adverse possession advanced against the property. In the ideal, this declaration should cover as long a period as possible to deal with rights and adverse possession that arose in the last decade.

In the case of this property, the vendors did provide a sworn declaration of possession that they have owned the property since the date of their purchase, and I enclose a copy for your files. I also requested that the vendors provide a copy of the declaration of possession that they received when they purchased the property. The previous owners were the parents of the female vendor and are thus easily accessible. I received an undertaking from the vendors solicitors to provide a new declaration of possession.

I confirm that you instructed us to close the transaction absent of an up to date survey if satisfactory declarations of possession were received. I will forward the declaration from the previous owners once it is received.

I trust that this matter has been handled to your satisfaction.

Yours truly,

Michael, Eliad & Redford

Robert B. Redford

rm

Encl.

Mr. and Mrs. Nicholas Cain
2 Brothers Road
Toronto, Ontario
M2W 6L6

869 SENECA LANE
TORONTO, ONTARIO
M6K 1F6

REFERENCE NO._____

IN ACCOUNT WITH

MICHAEL, ELIAD & REDFORD
BARRISTERS AND SOLICITORS

Re: Cain purchase from Abel
      2 Brothers Road, York

TO PROFESSIONAL SERVICES RENDERED:

To receiving and considering the agreement of purchase and sale: to conducting and reviewing searches on title and to drafting requisitions; to obtaining certificates of clearance from utilities, tax, and municipal authorities; to attendance at closing; to registering a transfer/ deed of land in your favour; to preparing, engrossing, and attending to the execution of a first charge mortgage in favour of the Dyss Trust Company, and registration there of; to all letters, telephone conversations, and attendances; to reporting to you the Dyss Trust Company.

OUR FEE _____
GST _____

Disbursements

Subject to GST

Paid for gas certificate	$10.70	
Paid for mileage and parking	29.55	
Paid to search title	50.00	
	$90.25	
GST	6.32	
		96.57

Not Subject to GST

Paid for City of York Certificates	$85.70	
Paid for hydro certificate	10.70	
		96.40

Carried forward	$1,958.47

STATEMENT OF ADJUSTMENTS
Solomon sale to King
100 Sisyphus Road, North York
Closing Date: _____

SALE PRICE   _____

DEPOSIT   _____

TAXES estimated at _____

Vendor paid   _____

Vendor's share for 96 days   _____

Allow vendor   _____   _____

FIRE INSURANCE-Purchaser to arrange own

BALANCE due on closing

Payable to Michael, Eliad & Redford   _____   _____

As per direction   _____   _____

E. & O.E.

MICHAEL, ELIAD & REDFORD
BARRISTERS AND SOLICITORS
869 SENECA LANE
TORONTO, ONTARIO M6K 1F6

JOSEPH A. MICHAEL
DAVID W. ELIAD
ROBERT B. REDFORD
MARGARET T NESH

REFERENCE NO._____

Today's Date

Castles & Sands
Barristers and Solicitors
Suite 900, 205 Portage Street
Markham, Ontario
L3R 3G3

Attention: Mr. Raymond G. Castles

Dear Mr. Castles:

Re: Soloman sale to King
      100 Sisyphus Road, North York, Lot 80, Plan 8090

We acknowledge receipt of your letter of requisitions. Accordingly, we would reply using your numbering system.

1.   Our clients will not provide that the fixtures and chattels are in good working order. They will provide that the fixtures and chattels are in the same condition as when inspected by your clients, fair wear and tear excepted.

2.   Our clients have provided in the agreement of purchase and sale only to remove any accumulated garbage.

3.   This provision should be the subject of a specific requisition and not a general and vague undertaking. If you are aware of any such encumbrances you have until the time set out in the agreement of purchase and sale to make valid requisitions. You have not done so.

4.   Our clients are not surveyors and have a simple obligation under the agreement of purchase and sale to produce a copy of the survey in their possession. We enclose it now. If your clients wish to pay for their own survey to confirm the points you raise, they may do so.

5. Please satisfy yourself wit regard to construction liens. The most that our clients will provide is a declaration that within the last sixty days there has been no activity carried out on the property that might give to a construction lien. Satisfy yourself with regard to executions.

We hereby deny your right to make further and other requisitions.

Yours truly,

Michael, Eliad & Redford

Robert B. Redford

rm

Encl.

CASTLES & SANDS
Barristers and Solicitors
Sutie 900, 205 Portage Street
Markham, Ontario L3R 3G3

Michael, Eliad & Redford
Barristers and Solicitors
869 Seneca Lane
Toronto, Ontario
M6K 1F6

Attention: Mr.B.Redford

Re: Abel sale to Cain
        2 Brothers Road, York, Lot 11, Plan 9614

Without admitting the validity of any of the requisitions contained in your letter of requisitions, and solely for the purpose of assisting you in the completion of this transaction, we answer your requisitions using the same numerical sequence as found in your letter of requisitions:

1.   A copy of the existing survey is enclosed, as per the agreement of purchase and sale.

2 and 3.   To be provided on closing.

4,5, and 6. Kindly satisfy yourself.

7. and 8.   Your form of bill of sale and warranties shall be provided on closing.

9.   Kindly satisfy yourself.

10.   Statement of adjustments is enclosed.

11.   Your form of bill and sale and warranties shall be provide on closing.

12.   Kindly satisfy yourself.

13.   The proper recital shall be inserted in the transfer/deed.

14.   Denied. The case you refer to was a motion brought under the Vendors and Purchasers Act, and is not of binding authority. If your clients wished to enter the premises prior to closing, such right should have been included in the agreement of purchase and sale.

15.   Your form of statutory declaration shall be provided on closing.

16.   We shall register a discharge of this charge/mortgage on or before closing.

We enclose a draft transfer/deed of land engrossed as per your letter regarding title, and we deny your right to submit any further requisitions.

Yours truly,

Castles & Sands

Raymond G. Castles

rm

Encl.

MICHAEL, ELIAD & REDFORD
BARRISTERS AND SOLICITORS
869 SENECA LANE
TORONTO, ONTARIO M6K 1F6

JOSEPH A. MICHAEL
DAVID W. ELIAD
ROBERT B. REDFORD
MARGARET T NESH

REFERENCE NO._____

Today's Date

Castles & Sands
Barristers and Solicitors
Suite 900
205 Portage Street
Markham, Ontario
L3R 3G3

Attention: Mr. Raymond G. Castles

Dear Mr. Castles:

Re: Cain purchase from Abel
       2 Brothers Road, York, Lot 11, Plan 9614

We have now completed our search of title in the above transaction and submit the following requisitions on title, without prejudice, to our clients' rights to make further and requisitions as many be required and without prejudice to our clients' rights under the terms of the agreement of purchase and sale reserving the right to modify or waive any or all of the requisitions here in:

1. REQUIRED: all or before closing, production and delivery of an original valid and up to date survey of the subject property.

2. REQUIRED: vacant possession and keys on closing or such other date as may be agreed upon by the parties.

3. REQUIRED: on or before closing, the production and registration of title of a valid discharge of any liens, charges/mortgages, and /or encumbrances whatsoever registered or unregistered, other than those charges/mortgages which may be assumed by our clients in accordance with the terms of the agreement of purchase and sale.

4. REQUIRED: on or before closing, evidence to show possession consistent with the registered title that the buildings presently located on the property are situated wholly with in the lot lines and erected in accordance with the appropriate statutes and by-laws of the municipality and any provincial or federal governmental agency having jurisdiction therein, and that there are no liens, charges, easements, right-of-way, rights of encumbrance which affect the property, or chattels and fixtures included in the sale, not disclosed by the registered title.

5. REQUIRED: on or before closing, evidence that there are no arrears of taxes or penalties for arrears of taxes or for water, hydro, gas, electricity, or oil with respect to the property

Although we will be making the usual searches for utility arrears, final readings will not take place until the closing date set out in the agreement of purchase and sale. Under the provisions of The Public Utilities Act, outstanding hydro, water, and gas accounts form a lien against the property and may be added as outstanding taxes and collected as tax arrears. We will, therefore, require on closing evidence that all utility accounts up to and including the date of closing have been paid in full. In the alternative, we will require your firms undertaking to retain sufficient funds from the proceeds of sale to pay any outstanding accounts that are the responsibility of your clients.

6. REQUIRED: evidence that there are no executions against the vendors or predecessors on title filed with the sheriff or Land Registry Office which may affect title to the property.

7. REQUIRED: evidence that the property is not and never has been insulated with urea formaldehyde foam insulation.

8. REQUIRED: evidence that the chattels included in the agreement of purchase and sale are fully paid for and are not subject to any liens or encumbrances and shall remain on the remises on closing and are in good working order.

9. REQUIRED: evidence that the present use of property may be continued and that there are no outstanding work orders or deficiency notices under any municipal by-law or provincial legislation affecting the property.

10. REQUIRED: prior to closing delivery of a statement of adjustments in duplicate, together with a direction as to the payment of funds, if required, and an undertaking to re-adjust the statement of adjustments, if necessary.

11. REQUIRED: on or before closing, evidence that the vendor is not a non-resident of Canada within the meaning of the Income Tax Act of Canada, or, in the alternative, evidence of the compliance with the act as required there in.

12. REQUIRED: on or before closing satisfactory evidence that the vendor ahs not contravened the provisions of the Planning Act, and amendments there to.

13. REQUIRED: evidence that the vendor has complied with the provisions the Family Law Act.

14. REQUIRED: that the purchasers, or their agents, be given the opportunity to inspect the premises on eh day of closing, pursuant to <u>Harkness v. Cooney and others,</u> 131 D.L.R. (3d) 765

15. REQUIRED: pursuant to the GST legislation, the execution, and the delivery on the closing of the GST certificate to be forwarded shortly. Please note that should the certificate be false, your client will be responsible for the resulting GST. If you claim that GST is payable by the purchaser, please advise immediately so that we may seek further instructions from our clients.

16. Instrument Number 123456 is a charge/mortgage in favour of Christian Vidaal and Christine Vidaal securing the amount of $150,000.00 and registered on _____.

17. REQUIRED: on or before closing, production and registration of a discharge of the said charge/mortgage of land.

Please be aware that since this charge/mortgage is not an institutional charge, we will not accept a solicitor's undertaking.

We enclose a form of undertaking, declaration of possession, bill of sale and warranties, and declaration regarding GST, in triplicate, which we would ask to have your clients execute and return to us in duplicate on or before closing.

Yours truly,

Michael, Eliad & Redford

Robert B. Redford
rm

Encl.

MICHAEL, ELIAD & REDFORD
BARRISTERS AND SOLICITORS
869 SENECA LANE
TORONTO, ONTARIO M6K 1F6

JOSEPH A. MICHAEL
DAVID W. ELIAD
ROBERT B. REDFORD
MARGARET T NESH

REFERENCE NO._____

Today's Date

Building Department
City of York
2700 Eglinton Avenue West
Toronto, Ontario
M6M 1V1

Ladies and Gentlemen,

Re: Cain purchase from Abel
        2 Brothers Road, York, Lot 11, Plan 9614

We act for the purchaser in the above transaction which closes on _____. Please advise us if the property complies with all applicable building and zoning requirements as set out in the by-laws governing the property, and specifically advise:

  (a)   if the land complies with lot area, lot frontage, and lot depth requirements;

  (b)   if the building complies with height, floor area, density, and set back requirements;

  (c)   if the use of the land as a single dwelling is permitted;

  (d)   if the municipal council has commenced procedures under the Planning Act to alter the zoning

  (e)   if there are outstanding work orders or notices against the property and if the building meets the municipal by-laws;

    (f)   if the subject property is a legal non-conforming use or if a minor variance hsas been granted.

We enclose a plan of survey of the property and our cheque in the amount of _____ to cover your fees.

Yours truly,

Michael, Elaid & Redford

Robert B. Redford

rm

Encl.

MICHAEL, ELIAD & REDFORD
BARRISTERS AND SOLICITORS
869 SENECA LANE
TORONTO, ONTARIO M6K 1F6

JOSEPH A. MICHAEL
DAVID W. ELIAD
ROBERT B. REDFORD
MARGARET T NESH

REFERENCE NO._____

Today's Date

Water Department
City of York
1652 Keele Street
Toronto, Ontario
M6M 3W4

Ladies and Gentlemen,

Re: Cain purchase from Abel
      2 Brothers Road, York, Lot 11, Plan 9614

We act for the purchasers in the above transaction which closes on _____. Please advise if there are any arrears for water rates charged to the property or if there is any equipment against which you have a claim.

Please arrange for the meter to be read on _____, and forward the final fill to Castles & Sands, Barristers and Solicitors, Suite 900, 205 Portage Street, Markham, Ontario, L3R 3G3, attention Mr. Raymond G. Castles. After _____, your records should be amended to show Mr. Nicholas and Mrs. Stephanie Cain as the new owners, and bills should be sent to them at the property address.

We enclose a cheque for _____ to cover your service fees.

Yours truly,

Michael, Eliad & Redford

rm

Encl.

DIRECTION REGARDING FUNDS

TO: Dyss Trust Company, first chargee

RE: Cain purchase from Abel, 2 Brothers Road, York, Lot 11, Plan 9614
                First Charge Mortgage, Loan No. 080101

You are authorized and directed to make the proceeds of the above transaction payable to our solicitors, Michael, Eliad & Redford, in trust, or to whom they may direct, and this shall be your good and sufficient authority for doing so.

Dated at Toronto on   , 200____.

_____
Nicholas Windsor Cain

_____
Stephanie Denise Cain

DIRECTION REGARDING TITILE

TO: Jason Abel and Jessica Abel, vendors

AND TO: Castles & Sands, solicitors for the vendors

RE: Cain purchase from Abel, 2 Brothers Road, York, Lot 11, Plan 9614

YOU ARE AUTHORIZED and directed to engross the title documents as follows, and this shall be your good and sufficient authority for doing so:

CAIN, Nicholas Windsor   Date of birth: June 16, 1966
CAIN, Stephanie Denise   Date of birth July 13, 1968

Dated at Toronto on   , 200____.

_____
Nicholas Windsor Cain

_____
Stephanie Denise Cain

UNDERTAKING

TO: Nicholas Windsor Cain and Stephanie Denise Cain, purchasers

AND TO: Michael, Eliad & Redford, solicitors for the purchasers

RE: Cain purchase from Abel, 2 Brothers Road, York, Lot 11, Plan 9614

In consideration of the closing of this transaction, we undertake as follows:

1. To pay all hydro, water, gas, and public utility accounts up to the date of closing and to supply and pay for fuel oil in accordance with the statement of adjustments

2. To re-adjust taxes if necessary and to pay any arrears of taxes and current taxes shown as paid in the statement of adjustments.

3. To re-adjust all errors and omissions on the statement of adjustments immediately upon written demand.

4. To pay insurance premiums as set out in the statement of adjustments.

5. To deliver up vacant possession of the above noted premised, together with all keys in he relation thereto on closing.

6. That there are no executions outstanding against us.

7. That we are non-residents of Canada within the meaning of section 116 of the Income Tax of Canada.

8. To pay all common expenses and maintenance charges shown as paid on the statement of adjustments.

Dated at Toronto on (Month)   , 200____.

_____
Jason Abel

_____
Jessica Abel

MICHAEL, ELIAD & REDFORD
BARRISTERS AND SOLICITORS
869 SENECA LANE
TORONTO, ONTARIO M6K 1F6

JOSEPH A. MICHAEL
DAVID W. ELIAD
ROBERT B. REDFORD
MARGARET T NESH

REFERENCE NO._____

Today's Date

Mr. and Mrs. Nicholas Cain
2 Brothers Road
Toronto, Ontario
M2W 6L6

Dear Mr. and Mrs. Cain:

RE: <u>Your purchase from Abel, 2 Brothers Road, York</u>

We have now completed your purchase of the above property and give you our report as follows:

<u>Transfer/Deed of Land</u>

The transfer/deed received on closing was registered as Instrument No. TB343434 in the name of Nicholas Windsor Cain and Stephanie Denise Cain, as joint tenants.

<u>Title</u>

I have examined the title to the said lands and, based on the examination of the documents in the transaction, we are of the opinion that you have a good and marketable title to the said lands and that title was, at the date of closing, free from encumbrance, save for any restrictions running with the lands and any defects or discrepancies revealed by the up to date survey and surveying matters generally, subject to any unknown liens under the Construction Lien Act.

<u>Subdivision Control</u>

The Planning Act makes it unlawful to subdivide any land in Ontario without consent pursuant to the statute. Title to abutting properties was searched, and no breach of the statute was discovered,

Executions

We have searched at the Sheriff's office and satisfied ourselves that at the time of closing, there were no executions affecting title to the said lands.

Statement of Adjustments

This transaction closed on (Insert Closing Date), as provided for the contract of sale, as amended by the parties, and adjustments were made as of that date.

The amount due on closing according to the statement of adjustments, a copy of which is enclosed, was $205 198.19.

By reference of the statement of adjustments, you will see that you were given credit for the deposit of $10 0000.00 paid to the real estate agency to be held in an interest bearing account. The interest was to be credited to you as soon as possible after closing.

The certificate of the Treasurer of the City of York certifies that there are arrears of taxes. The vendor provided proof that certain tax payments had been made and a solicitor's undertaking to hold back sufficient funds to cover tax arrears. Should they not be paid. The vendor was allowed the sum of $198.19, being the overpayment for the period from the closing date to the end of the calendar year. You should check with the City of York to ensure that future payments are made in a timely manner and you don not incur penalties.

Payment of realty taxes is the responsibility of the owner whether or not a tax bill is received. Please check the municipal offices to ensure that your ownership is noted in the municipal records.

No current adjustment was necessary for hydro as payment is calculated on consumption measured by a meter.

Chattels

The contract of sale provided that the purchase price included the purchase of a number of older model appliances, namely, fridge, stove, dryer, broadloom where laid, electric light fixtures, oil burner and equipment.

Mr. and Mrs. Nicholas Cain
Page 3
Today's Date

Retail Sales Tax

Responsibility for the payment of any retail sales tax on the purchase of the chattels falls initially on the purchaser. No value was assigned to these chattels in your land transfer tax affidavit, so no retail sales tax was paid at the time of the registration of your transfer/deed.

Land Transfer Tax

We paid land transfer tax in the amount of $1 875.00 and the registration fee of $50/00 from the funds deposited to your credit in our trust account.

First Charge/Mortgage

Your title to the said lands to subject to a first charge/mortgage in favour of the Dyss Trust Company which was arranged and executed by you and which secures the sum of $182 750.00 with interest rate of 6.7 percent per year.

The charge/mortgage is payable monthly in the amount of $1 375.00 which included principal and interest on the 17th day of each and every month, in each and every year, to and including the 17th day of (Closing Date), and the balance, if any, is payable on the date last mentioned.

The first payment of principal and interest falls due on the 17th day of (Month) (Year). Payments aer to be made in favour of the Dyss Trust Company by direct deduction from your bank account.

The charge/mortgage is conventional in all respects the subject to a CMHC guarantee. In order to secure the CMHC guarantee, you paid a fee directly to the Dyss Trust Company.

Insurance

No adjustments was made as you were to arrange your own insurance.

The premises are insured by Prometheus Insurance Company, Binder No. 32025 with coverage for one year commencing at the date of closing, with loss payable to the Dyss Trust Company, as its interests may appear. If you have not already done so, you will soon receive a copy of the policy from your broker. While property is subject to charge/mortgage, it will be necessary for you to satisfy the charge/mortgagee as to adequate insurance coverage and as to the protection of the interest chargee/mortgagee.

Plan of Survey

The vendors' solicitor supplied a plan of survey sufficient for financing purposes, which plan of survey was made by Oscar Chip, O.L.S., and was dated June 3, 1927. The plan indicates that the buildings are wholly within the lot lines. The extreme age of the survey was discussed with you and you instructed us not to order an up-to-date survey, despi9te our advice that our opinion as to title would be limited. You received on closing a statutory declaration from the vendors stating that they have reviewed the survey. We also received an undertaking from the vendors' solicitors to provide similar declaration from the previous owners. Such declarations provide some evidence that there has been no claim for adverse possession encroachments on the property since the survey was prepared.

Since the building was completed before the enactment of the zoning by-laws, the building would, if there were any violations or alterations must be made in compliance with the by-laws in effect on their completion and pursuant to a valid building permit.

Family Law Act

The vendors completed a statement pursuant to the Family Law Act stating facts which indicate compliance with that act.

Land Transfer Tax Act

Since you aer a permanent resident of Canada, you were able to complete an affidavit to that effect.

Insulaltion

The vendors delivered on closing a warranty with respect to the Urea Formaldehyde Foam Insulation (UFFI). This warranty states that the property has never been insulated with UFFI.

Enclosures

Please find enclosed:

1. Registered duplicate transfer deed.

2. Copy of charge/mortgage.

3. Set of standard charge terms.

4. Copy of the amortization schedule for the Dyss Trust Company charge/mortgage.

5. Copy of certificate of City of York, Hydro and Water Revenue.

6. Copy of certificate of City of York, Building Department.

7. Copy of certificate of Consumers Gas.

8. Executed copy of direction regarding funds.

9. Executed undertaking, declaration of possession, bill of sale and warranties, and declaration as to G.S.T. exemption.

10. Copy of the statement of adjustments.

11. Copy of execution certificate.

Account

We also enclose our account and ledger statement which show you how we handled the money on closing.

Thank you for giving us the opportunity to serve you in the purchase of your new home. Please call us with any questions.

Yours truly,

MICHAEL, ELIAD & REDFORD

Robert B. Redford

rm

Encl.